EAGLE BRAND

Cookies & Treats

65 EASY RECIPES

Publications International, Ltd.
Favorite Brand Name Recipes at www.fbnr.com

Photography: All photographs *except* those on pages 6, 7 and 9 by Peter Walters Photography/Chicago
Photographers: Peter Walters, Cindy Trim
Photographers' Assistant: Chris Lake
Prop Stylist: Sally Grimes
Food Stylists: Janice Bell, Kim Hartman
Assistant Food Stylist: Vanessa Dubiel

Pictured on the front cover *(clockwise from top):* Chocolate Chip Treasure Cookie *(page 13),* Cookies 'n' Crème Fudge *(page 60),* Double Chocolate Brownie *(page 38)* and Magic Cookie Bar *(page 18).*

Pictured on the back cover *(clockwise from top):* Crunchy Clusters *(page 53),* Peanut Blossom Cookies *(page 52)* and Easy Peanut Butter Cookies *(page 52);* Creamy Baked Cheesecake *(page 12);* Party Mints *(page 79)* and Festive Cranberry Cream Punch *(page 78).*

ISBN: 0-7853-4591-4

Manufactured in China.

8 7 6 5 4 3 2 1

Microwave Cooking: Microwave ovens vary in wattage. Use the cooking times as guidelines and check for doneness before adding more time.

Preparation/Cooking Times: Preparation times are based on the approximate amount of time required to assemble the recipe before cooking, baking, chilling or serving. These times include preparation steps such as measuring, chopping and mixing. The fact that some preparations and cooking can be done simultaneously is taken into account. Preparation of optional ingredients and serving suggestions is not included.

EAGLE BRAND
Cookies & Treats

65 EASY RECIPES

The Magic of Eagle® Brand

For over 144 years, Eagle Brand has been America's #1 trusted brand of sweetened condensed milk. Since 1856, bakers have been depending on all-natural Eagle® Brand Sweetened Condensed Milk to help them make all kinds of indulgent desserts and sweet treats. There are three varieties of Eagle Brand: Original, introduced in 1856; Low Fat, introduced in 1994; and Fat Free, introduced in 1995. All three provide the rich, creamy, sweet taste that's the delicious secret to making fabulous desserts, candies, beverages and treats. Eagle Brand has been developing and creating deliciously foolproof recipes for decades.

THE MAGIC INGREDIENT

Beginners and experienced cooks alike love making treats with Eagle Brand because it guarantees success. It is a special blend of milk and sugar that is condensed by a unique vacuum process to create a "foolproof" base for a variety of recipes. Many recipes that use Eagle Brand require no additional sugar because it contains sugar that has been thoroughly dissolved during manufacturing, resulting in timesaving steps. Eagle Brand has a magical thickening quality too. When it is combined with acidic fruit juice, such as lemon, lime or orange juice, it thickens—without heating—to form rich and creamy pie fillings, puddings and cheesecakes. When heated with chocolate, Eagle Brand quickly thickens to a velvety smooth consistency for candies and sauces that are never grainy or long-cooking. Remember: Evaporated milk is completely different than Eagle Brand and cannot be substituted for it.

MAKE MAGIC IN MINUTES

There's no easier way to bring magic into your day than with Eagle Brand. Turn the pages of this publication and you'll find a variety of recipes perfect to make any time of year. There are holiday favorites like Traditional Pumpkin Pie and Peanut Blossom Cookies, as well as any-day treats like Magic Cookie Bars and Double Chocolate Brownies. Marbled Cheesecake Bars are a great way to end a spring luncheon, and Key Lime Pie is

Magic Cookie Bars, page 18

refreshing on a hot summer afternoon. There are even fabulous no-bake recipes for those days when just the thought of turning on the oven is too much to bear. So whether you're craving a classic Eagle Brand treat, like Foolproof Dark Chocolate Fudge, or you want to try something new, like Deep Dish Mocha Tiramisu, with these recipes and Eagle Brand, you'll be making magic in minutes!

EAGLE® BRAND ON THE INTERNET

For more information and recipes using Eagle® Brand Sweetened Condensed Milk, visit our website at www.eaglebrand.com.

HINTS FOR USING EAGLE BRAND

KEEPING IT FRESH
Store unopened cans of Eagle Brand in a cool dry place—not near the range. Because it is a natural product, Eagle Brand may vary in color and consistency from can to can. It will become thicker and more caramel-colored when kept on the shelf for a long time. These changes will not affect its quality, simply stir briskly before using. If you don't need the whole can for a recipe, measure the desired amount and place the remainder in a glass or plastic storage container. Cover it tightly and keep it in the refrigerator. It will stay fresh about one week.

MELTING CHOCOLATE
Chocolate melts smoothly and easily with Eagle Brand. For the smoothest texture, be sure to use a medium to heavy saucepan and low heat. As the chocolate heats, stir the mixture constantly until it is smooth. If the heat is too high, the chocolate may form tiny clumps.

MAKING CARAMEL

For an easy caramel topping or dip, simply heat Eagle Brand and serve it over ice cream or with assorted cookies and fruit. Just follow one of these easy methods:

© The Borden Company 1940

Oven: Preheat the oven to 425°F. Pour 1 can Eagle Brand into a 9-inch pie plate. Cover with foil; place in a larger shallow pan. Fill the larger pan with hot water. Bake 1 hour or until Eagle Brand is thick and caramel-colored. Beat until smooth.

Stovetop: Pour 1 can Eagle Brand into the top of a double boiler; place over boiling water. Over low heat, simmer 1 to 1½ hours or until thick and caramel-colored, stirring occasionally. Beat until smooth.

Microwave: Pour 1 can Eagle Brand into a 2-quart microwave-safe glass measuring cup. Cook on 50% power (MEDIUM) 4 minutes, stirring briskly every 2 minutes until smooth. Cook on 30% power (MEDIUM-LOW) 20 to 26 minutes or until very thick and caramel-colored. Stir briskly every 4 minutes during the first 16 minutes, and every 2 minutes during the last 4 to 10 minutes. *Caution: Never heat an unopened can.*

GIFT GIVING MADE EASY

Homemade treats become gorgeous gifts when arranged in unique packages wrapped in festive papers and decorated with ribbons or bows. Show someone how much you care by wrapping delicious Eagle Brand treats in fun, festive containers from around the house.

Easy Chocolate Truffles, page 71

Plates & Bowls: Choose a festive plate, tray or bowl—from paper, to crockery, to the fanciest china— then stack the sweets high and wrap it all up with clear or colored plastic wrap or cellophane. Attach some pretty ribbons or a big bow and the gift is ready for giving.

Boxes & Tins: Boxes and tins come in a variety of shapes and sizes and are the perfect containers for cookies, bars and candies. Line the box or tin with tissue paper and then fill with tasty goodies. For a special touch, tuck candies or small cookies into colored paper or foil liners before placing them in the container.

Baskets: Baskets are versatile and are available in a large array of shapes, sizes and materials. Simply line the basket with pretty paper or cloth napkins and pile in the treats.

Glass Jars: Large, wide-mouthed canning jars are great for dessert sauces. Fill them to the brim and slip rounds of colorful cloth between the lids and the metal screw bands.

9

Irresistible Classics

*W*ho can resist Magic Cookie Bars, Chocolate Chip Treasure Cookies or Foolproof Dark Chocolate Fudge? No one can! These are just a few of the Eagle® Brand classics that have been loved by families for generations. Try one of these fabulous bars, sensational cookies or spectacular desserts and you'll discover how Eagle® Brand "Makes Magic in Minutes." We've even included some fun variations so you can create a new twist on your favorite classic. Creamy Baked Cheesecake, Lemon Crumb Bars—the list of favorites goes on and on!

Creamy Baked Cheesecake (page 12)

Creamy Baked Cheesecake

Prep Time: 25 minutes   **Bake Time:** 55 to 60 minutes

  1¼ cups graham cracker crumbs
  ¼ cup sugar
  ⅓ cup (⅔ stick) butter or margarine, melted
  2 (8-ounce) packages cream cheese, softened
  1 (14-ounce) can Eagle® Brand Sweetened Condensed Milk (NOT evaporated milk)
  3 eggs
  ¼ cup ReaLemon® Lemon Juice from Concentrate
  1 (8-ounce) container sour cream, at room temperature
    Raspberry Topping (recipe follows, optional)

1. Preheat oven to 300°F. Combine crumbs, sugar and butter; press firmly on bottom of ungreased 9-inch springform pan.

2. In large bowl, beat cream cheese until fluffy.

3. Gradually beat in **Eagle Brand** until smooth. Add eggs and **ReaLemon;** mix well. Pour into prepared pan.

4. Bake 50 to 55 minutes or until set.

5. Remove from oven; top with sour cream. Bake 5 minutes longer. Cool. Chill. Prepare Raspberry Topping and serve with cheesecake. Store covered in refrigerator.   *Makes 1 (9-inch) cheesecake*

Raspberry Topping

Prep Time: 5 minutes

  1 (10-ounce) package thawed frozen red raspberries in syrup
  ¼ cup red currant jelly or red raspberry jam
  1 tablespoon cornstarch

1. Drain ⅔ cup syrup from raspberries.

2. In small saucepan over medium heat, combine syrup, jelly and cornstarch. Cook and stir until slightly thickened and clear. Cool. Stir in raspberries.

New York Style Cheesecake: Increase cream cheese to 4 (8-ounce) packages and eggs to 4. Proceed as directed, adding 2 tablespoons flour after eggs. Bake 1 hour 10 minutes or until center is set. Omit sour cream. Cool. Chill. Serve and store as directed.

Chocolate Chip Treasure Cookies

Prep Time: 15 minutes   **Bake Time:** 9 to 10 minutes

  1½ cups graham cracker crumbs
   ½ cup all-purpose flour
    2 teaspoons baking powder
    1 (14-ounce) can Eagle® Brand Sweetened Condensed Milk (NOT evaporated milk)
   ½ cup (1 stick) butter or margarine, softened
  1⅓ cups flaked coconut
    1 (12-ounce) package semi-sweet chocolate chips
    1 cup chopped walnuts

1. Preheat oven to 375°F. In small bowl, combine crumbs, flour and baking powder.

2. In large bowl, beat **Eagle Brand** and butter until smooth. Add crumb mixture; mix well. Stir in coconut, chips and walnuts.

3. Drop by rounded tablespoons onto ungreased cookie sheets. Bake 9 to 10 minutes or until lightly browned. Store loosely covered at room temperature.   *Makes about 3 dozen*

Double Delicious Cookie Bars

Prep Time: 10 minutes   **Bake Time:** 25 to 30 minutes

½ cup (1 stick) butter or margarine
1½ cups graham cracker crumbs
1 (14-ounce) can Eagle® Brand Sweetened Condensed Milk (NOT evaporated milk)
2 cups (12 ounces) semi-sweet chocolate chips*
1 cup (6 ounces) peanut butter-flavored chips*

Butterscotch-flavored chips or white chocolate chips may be substituted for the semi-sweet chocolate chips and/or peanut butter chips.

1. Preheat oven to 350°F (325°F for glass dish). In 13×9-inch baking pan, melt butter in oven.

2. Sprinkle crumbs evenly over butter; pour **Eagle Brand** evenly over crumbs. Top with remaining ingredients; press down firmly.

3. Bake 25 to 30 minutes or until lightly browned. Cool. Cut into bars. Store covered at room temperature.   *Makes 24 to 36 bars*

 *Helpful Hint*

For perfectly cut bars, line the entire pan with a sheet of aluminum foil first. When the bars are baked and have cooled, lift up the edges of the foil to remove the bars from the pan. Cut into individual squares, rectangles, triangles or diamonds and peel off the foil.

Double Delicious Cookie Bars

Foolproof Dark Chocolate Fudge

Prep Time: 10 minutes   **Chill Time:** 2 hours

   3 cups (18 ounces) semi-sweet chocolate chips
   1 (14-ounce) can Eagle® Brand Sweetened Condensed Milk (NOT evaporated milk)
   Dash of salt
   ½ to 1 cup chopped nuts (optional)
 1½ teaspoons vanilla extract

1. Line 8- or 9-inch square pan with foil. Butter foil; set aside.

2. In heavy saucepan over low heat, melt chips with **Eagle Brand** and salt. Remove from heat; stir in nuts and vanilla. Spread evenly in prepared pan.

3. Chill 2 hours or until firm. Turn fudge onto cutting board; peel off foil and cut into squares. Store covered in refrigerator.

Makes about 2 pounds

Marshmallow Fudge: Stir in 2 tablespoons butter with vanilla. Substitute 2 cups miniature marshmallows for nuts. Proceed as directed above.

Foolproof Dark Chocolate Fudge

Magic Cookie Bars

Prep Time: 10 minutes   **Bake Time:** 25 minutes

> ½ cup (1 stick) butter or margarine
> 1½ cups graham cracker crumbs
> 1 (14-ounce) can Eagle® Brand Sweetened Condensed Milk (NOT evaporated milk)
> 2 cups (12 ounces) semi-sweet chocolate chips
> 1⅓ cups flaked coconut
> 1 cup chopped nuts

1. Preheat oven to 350°F (325°F for glass dish). In 13×9-inch baking pan, melt butter in oven.

2. Sprinkle crumbs over butter; pour **Eagle Brand** evenly over crumbs. Layer evenly with remaining ingredients; press down firmly.

3. Bake 25 minutes or until lightly browned. Cool. Chill if desired. Cut into bars. Store loosely covered at room temperature.

Makes 24 to 36 bars

7-Layer Magic Cookie Bars: Substitute 1 cup (6 ounces) butterscotch-flavored chips* for 1 cup semi-sweet chocolate chips and proceed as directed above.

*Peanut butter-flavored chips or white chocolate chips may be substituted for butterscotch-flavored chips.

Magic Peanut Cookie Bars: Substitute 2 cups (about ¾ pound) chocolate-covered peanuts for semi-sweet chocolate chips and chopped nuts.

Magic Rainbow Cookie Bars: Substitute 2 cups plain candy-coated chocolate candies for semi-sweet chocolate chips.

Top to bottom: 7-Layer Magic Cookie Bars and Magic Rainbow Cookie Bars

Magic Make It Your Way Drop Cookies

Prep Time: 15 minutes   **Bake Time:** 8 to 10 minutes

> 3 cups sifted all-purpose flour
> 3 teaspoons baking powder
> ¾ teaspoon salt
> ¾ cup (1½ sticks) butter or margarine, softened
> 2 eggs
> 1 teaspoon vanilla extract
> 1 (14-ounce) can Eagle® Brand Sweetened Condensed Milk (NOT evaporated milk)
> One "favorite" ingredient (see below)

1. Preheat oven to 350°F. Grease baking sheets; set aside. In large bowl, sift together dry ingredients. Stir in butter, eggs, vanilla and **Eagle Brand.** Fold in one of your "favorite" ingredients.

2. Drop by level teaspoonfuls, about 2 inches apart, onto prepared baking sheets. Bake 8 to 10 minutes or until edges are slightly browned. Remove at once from baking sheet. Cool. Store covered at room temperature.   *Makes about 4 dozen*

"Make it your way" with your favorite ingredient (pick one):
1 (6-ounce) package semi-sweet chocolate chips
1½ cups raisins
1½ cups corn flakes
1½ cups toasted shredded coconut

*Top to bottom: Magic Make It Your Way
Drop Cookies and Versatile Cut-Out
Cookies (page 22)*

Versatile Cut-Out Cookies

Prep Time: 15 minutes   **Bake Time:** 7 to 9 minutes

    3⅓ cups all-purpose flour
    1 tablespoon baking powder
    ½ teaspoon salt
    1 (14-ounce) can Eagle® Brand Sweetened Condensed Milk (NOT
        evaporated milk)
    ¾ cup (1½ sticks) butter or margarine, softened
    2 eggs
    2 teaspoons vanilla *or* 1½ teaspoons almond or lemon extract
        Ready-to-spread frosting

1. Preheat oven to 350°F. Grease baking sheets; set aside. In medium bowl, combine flour, baking powder and salt; set aside. In large bowl, beat **Eagle Brand,** butter, eggs and vanilla until well blended. Add dry ingredients; mix well.

2. On floured surface, lightly knead dough to form smooth ball. Divide into thirds. On well-floured surface, roll out each portion to ⅛-inch thickness. Cut with floured cookie cutter. Place 1 inch apart on prepared sheets.

3. Bake 7 to 9 minutes or until lightly browned around edges. Cool completely. Frost and decorate as desired. Store loosely covered at room temperature.   *Makes about 6½ dozen*

Sandwich Cookies: Use 2½-inch cookie cutter. Bake as directed above. Sandwich two cookies together with ready-to-spread frosting. Sprinkle with powdered sugar or colored sugar if desired. Makes about 3 dozen.

Traditional Pumpkin Pie

Prep Time: 20 minutes   **Bake Time:** 50 to 55 minutes

> 1 (15-ounce) can pumpkin (2 cups)
> 1 (14-ounce) can Eagle® Brand Sweetened Condensed Milk (NOT evaporated milk)
> 2 eggs
> 1 teaspoon ground cinnamon
> ½ teaspoon ground ginger
> ½ teaspoon ground nutmeg
> ½ teaspoon salt
> 1 (9-inch) unbaked pie crust
>   Favorite Topping (recipes follow, optional)

1. Preheat oven to 425°F. In large bowl, combine all ingredients except pie crust; mix well.

2. Pour into prepared pie crust. Bake 15 minutes.

3. Reduce oven heat to 350°F. Continue baking 35 to 40 minutes, or as directed with one Favorite Topping or, until knife inserted 1 inch from edge comes out clean. Cool. Garnish as desired. Store covered in refrigerator.   *Makes 1 (9-inch) pie*

Favorite Toppings

Sour Cream Topping: In medium bowl, combine 1½ cups sour cream, 2 tablespoons sugar and 1 teaspoon vanilla extract. After pie has baked 30 minutes at 350°F, spread evenly over top; bake 10 minutes.

Streusel Topping: In medium bowl, combine ½ cup packed brown sugar and ½ cup all-purpose flour; cut in ¼ cup (½ stick) cold butter or margarine until crumbly. Stir in ¼ cup chopped nuts. After pie has baked 30 minutes at 350°F, sprinkle evenly over top; bake 10 minutes.

Chocolate Glaze: In small saucepan over low heat, melt ½ cup semi-sweet chocolate chips and 1 teaspoon solid shortening. Drizzle or spread over top of baked and cooled pie.

Key Lime Pie

Prep Time: 25 minutes **Bake Time:** 45 minutes

Cool Time: 1 hour **Chill Time:** 3 hours

> **3 eggs, separated**
> **1 (14-ounce) can Eagle® Brand Sweetened Condensed Milk (NOT evaporated milk)**
> **½ cup ReaLime® Lime Juice from Concentrate**
> **2 to 3 drops green food coloring (optional)**
> **1 (9-inch) unbaked pie crust**
> **½ teaspoon cream of tartar**
> **⅓ cup sugar**

1. Preheat oven to 325°F. In medium bowl, beat egg yolks; gradually beat in **Eagle Brand** and **ReaLime.** Stir in food coloring. Pour into pie crust.

2. Bake 30 minutes. Remove from oven. Increase oven temperature to 350°F.

3. Meanwhile, for meringue, with clean mixer, beat egg whites and cream of tartar to soft peaks. Gradually beat in sugar, 1 tablespoon at a time. Beat 4 minutes or until stiff, glossy peaks form and sugar is dissolved.

4. Immediately spread meringue over hot pie, carefully sealing to edge of crust to prevent meringue from shrinking. Bake 15 minutes. Cool 1 hour. Chill at least 3 hours. Store covered in refrigerator.

Makes 8 servings

Key Lime Pie

Lemon Crumb Bars

Prep Time: 30 minutes   **Bake Time:** 35 minutes

1 (18¼-ounce) package lemon or yellow cake mix
½ cup (1 stick) butter or margarine, softened
1 egg plus 3 egg yolks
2 cups finely crushed saltine crackers (¼ pound)
1 (14-ounce) can Eagle® Brand Sweetened Condensed Milk (NOT
   evaporated milk)
½ cup ReaLemon® Lemon Juice from Concentrate

1. Preheat oven to 350°F. Grease 15×10×1-inch baking pan. In large bowl, combine cake mix, butter and 1 egg; mix well (mixture will be crumbly). Stir in cracker crumbs. Reserve 2 cups crumb mixture. Press remaining crumb mixture firmly on bottom of prepared pan. Bake 15 minutes.

2. Meanwhile, in medium bowl, combine egg yolks, **Eagle Brand** and **ReaLemon;** mix well. Spread evenly over baked crust.

3. Top with reserved crumb mixture. Bake 20 minutes or until firm. Cool. Cut into bars. Store covered in refrigerator.

Makes 36 to 48 bars

Helpful Hint

> *Here's a quick and easy way to make cracker or cookie crumbs: place crackers in a large resealable plastic food storage bag; seal. Roll a rolling pin over the crackers to crush.*

Lemon Crumb Bars

Fast 'n' Fabulous

*U*nexpected company dropping by? A merry group of little elves suddenly appearing on your doorstep? No problem! Any time you need a treat in a hurry, you can whip up one of the delicious beverages, outstanding bars and cookies or wonderful desserts in this chapter. And you can prepare these desserts in just 15 minutes or less! Eagle® Brand treats taste great, are easy to make, and are sure to satisfy all your guests. So fast and fabulous you'll think they're magic. Be careful. Your guests may never want to leave.

28   *Fudgy Milk Chocolate Fondue (page 30)*

Fudgy Milk Chocolate Fondue

Prep Time: 12 to 15 minutes

> 1 (16-ounce) can chocolate-flavored syrup
> 1 (14-ounce) can Eagle® Brand Sweetened Condensed Milk (NOT evaporated milk)
> Dash salt
> 1½ teaspoons vanilla extract
> Dippers: fresh fruit, cookies, pound cake cubes, angel food cake cubes

1. In heavy saucepan over medium heat, combine syrup, **Eagle Brand** and salt. Cook and stir 12 to 15 minutes or until slightly thickened.

2. Remove from heat; stir in vanilla. Serve warm with Dippers. Store covered in refrigerator.   *Makes about 3 cups*

Microwave Directions: In 1-quart glass measure, combine syrup, **Eagle Brand** and salt. Cook on 100% power (HIGH) 3½ to 4 minutes, stirring after 2 minutes. Stir in vanilla.

Tip: Can be served warm or cold over ice cream. Can be made several weeks ahead. Store tightly covered in refrigerator.

Chocolate-Topped Raspberry Cheese Pie

Prep Time: 15 minutes   Bake Time: 30 to 35 minutes

> **2 (3-ounce) packages cream cheese, softened**
> **1 (14-ounce) can Eagle® Brand Sweetened Condensed Milk (NOT evaporated milk)**
> **1 egg**
> **3 tablespoons ReaLemon® Lemon Juice from Concentrate**
> **1 teaspoon vanilla extract**
> **1 cup fresh or frozen raspberries**
> **1 (6-ounce) ready-made chocolate crumb pie crust**
> **Chocolate Glaze (recipe follows)**

1. Preheat oven to 350°F. In medium bowl, beat cream cheese until fluffy. Gradually beat in **Eagle Brand** until smooth. Add egg, **ReaLemon** and vanilla; mix well.

2. Arrange raspberries on bottom of crust. Slowly pour cheese mixture over fruit.

3. Bake 30 to 35 minutes or until center is almost set. Cool.

4. Prepare Chocolate Glaze and spread over cheesecake; chill. Garnish as desired. Store covered in refrigerator.   *Makes 1 pie*

Chocolate Glaze
In small saucepan over low heat, melt 2 (1-ounce) squares semi-sweet chocolate with ¼ cup whipping cream. Cook and stir until thickened and smooth. Remove from heat; cool slightly.

 *Helpful Hint*

To soften cream cheese quickly, unwrap 8 ounces of cream cheese and place on a microwave-safe plate. Microwave on 50% power (MEDIUM) 1 to 1½ minutes or until cream cheese is soft.

White Chocolate Squares

Prep Time: 15 minutes   **Bake Time:** 20 to 25 minutes

> 1 (12-ounce) package white chocolate chips, divided
> ¼ cup (½ stick) butter or margarine
> 2 cups all-purpose flour
> ½ teaspoon baking powder
> 1 (14-ounce) can Eagle® Brand Sweetened Condensed Milk (NOT evaporated milk)
> 1 cup chopped pecans, toasted
> 1 large egg
> 1 teaspoon vanilla extract
> Powdered sugar

1. Preheat oven to 350°F. Grease 13×9-inch baking pan. In large saucepan over low heat, melt 1 cup chips and butter. Stir in flour and baking powder until blended. Stir in **Eagle Brand,** pecans, egg, vanilla and remaining chips. Spoon mixture into prepared pan.

2. Bake 20 to 25 minutes. Cool. Sprinkle with powdered sugar; cut into squares. Store covered at room temperature.   *Makes 24 bars*

 *Helpful Hint*

> *Toasted nuts and coconut give foods a pleasant crunchiness and enhance the food's nutty flavor. To toast, spread the chopped nuts or coconut in a single layer in a shallow baking pan. Preheat the oven to 350°F. Bake 5 to 10 minutes or until light golden brown, stirring frequently to prevent burning.*

White Chocolate Squares

Homemade Cream Liqueurs

Prep Time: 5 minutes

> 1 (14-ounce) can Eagle® Brand Sweetened Condensed Milk (NOT evaporated milk)
> 1¼ cups flavored liqueur (almond, coffee, orange or mint)
> 2 cups (1 pint) whipping cream or coffee cream

1. In blender container, combine all ingredients; blend until smooth.

2. To serve, pour into glasses over ice. Garnish as desired. Store tightly covered in refrigerator. Stir before serving.

Makes about 1 quart

Chocolate Swizzle Nog

Prep Time: 5 minutes

> 2 cups milk
> 1 (14-ounce) can Eagle® Brand Sweetened Condensed Milk (NOT evaporated milk)
> 2 tablespoons unsweetened cocoa powder
> ½ teaspoon vanilla or peppermint extract
> Whipped cream or whipped topping

1. In medium saucepan over medium heat, combine milk, **Eagle Brand** and cocoa. Heat through, stirring constantly. Remove from heat; stir in vanilla.

2. Serve warm in mugs; top with whipped cream. Store covered in refrigerator.

Makes 4 servings

*Left to right: Homemade Cream Liqueur
and Chocolate Swizzle Nog*

Chocolate, Chocolate, Chocolate

Aahh, the sweet indulgence of rich, creamy chocolate. For anyone with a true passion for chocolate, the very mention of the word can cause shivers of delight and anticipation. Let your chocolate dreams come true with Eagle® Brand, the magic ingredient for foolproof, richly satisfying bars, decadent pies or melt-in-your-mouth confections. These and other Eagle® Brand recipes found in this chapter are sure to send any chocoholic to chocolate heaven!

Top to bottom: Double Chocolate Brownies (page 38) and Rocky Road Candy (page 39)

Double Chocolate Brownies

Prep Time: 15 minutes   **Bake Time:** 35 minutes

1¼ cups all-purpose flour, divided
¼ cup sugar
½ cup (1 stick) cold butter or margarine
1 (14-ounce) can Eagle® Brand Sweetened Condensed Milk (NOT
    evaporated milk)
¼ cup unsweetened cocoa
1 egg
1 teaspoon vanilla extract
½ teaspoon baking powder
1 (8-ounce) milk chocolate bar, broken into chunks
¾ cup chopped nuts (optional)

1. Preheat oven to 350°F. Line 13×9-inch baking pan with foil; set aside.

2. In medium bowl, combine 1 cup flour and sugar; cut in butter until crumbly. Press firmly on bottom of prepared pan. Bake 15 minutes.

3. In large bowl, beat **Eagle Brand,** cocoa, egg, remaining ¼ cup flour, vanilla and baking powder. Stir in chocolate chunks and nuts. Spread over baked crust. Bake 20 minutes or until set.

4. Cool. Use foil to lift out of pan. Cut into bars. Store tightly covered at room temperature.   *Makes 24 brownies*

Rocky Road Candy

Prep Time: 10 minutes   **Chill Time:** 2 hours

> 1 (12-ounce) package semi-sweet chocolate chips
> 2 tablespoons butter or margarine
> 1 (14-ounce) can Eagle® Brand Sweetened Condensed Milk (NOT evaporated milk)
> 2 cups dry roasted peanuts
> 1 (10½-ounce) package miniature marshmallows

1. Line 13×9-inch baking pan with waxed paper. In heavy saucepan over low heat, melt chips and butter with **Eagle Brand;** remove from heat.

2. In large bowl, combine peanuts and marshmallows; stir in chocolate mixture. Spread in prepared pan. Chill 2 hours or until firm.

3. Remove candy from pan; peel off paper and cut into squares. Store loosely covered at room temperature.

Makes about 3½ dozen

Microwave Directions: In 1-quart glass measure, combine chips, butter and **Eagle Brand.** Cook on 100% power (HIGH) 3 minutes, stirring after 1½ minutes. Stir to melt chips. Let stand 5 minutes. Proceed as directed above.

 *Helpful Hint*

> *For a more festive look, try cutting bars and candies into different shapes, such as rectangles, triangles or diamonds. To make diamonds, cut straight lines 1 to 1½ inches apart down the length of the bars. Then, diagonally cut straight lines 1 to 1½ inches apart across the bars.*

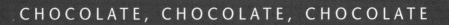

Chocolate Chiffon Pie

Prep Time: 20 minutes   **Chill Time:** 3 hours

- 2 (1-ounce) squares unsweetened chocolate, chopped
- 1 (14-ounce) can Eagle® Brand Sweetened Condensed Milk (NOT evaporated milk)
- 1 envelope unflavored gelatin
- ⅓ cup water
- ½ teaspoon vanilla extract
- 1 cup (½ pint) whipping cream, whipped
- 1 (6-ounce) ready-made chocolate or graham cracker crumb pie crust
- Additional whipped cream

1. In heavy saucepan over low heat, melt chocolate with **Eagle Brand.** Remove from heat.

2. Meanwhile, in small saucepan, sprinkle gelatin over water; let stand 1 minute. Over low heat, stir until gelatin dissolves.

3. Stir gelatin into chocolate mixture. Add vanilla. Cool to room temperature. Fold in whipped cream. Spread into crust.

4. Chill 3 hours or until set. Garnish with additional whipped cream. Store covered in refrigerator. *Makes 1 pie*

 *Helpful Hint*

For easy pie-making, nothing beats a ready-made pie crust and Eagle Brand! You'll find graham cracker and chocolate-flavored crumb crusts as well as pastry mixes in 1- and 2-crust sizes in the baking aisle of most supermarkets.

Chocolate Chiffon Pie

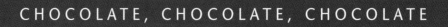

Fudge Ribbon Sheet Cake

Prep Time: 20 minutes   **Bake Time:** 40 minutes

1 (18¼-ounce) package chocolate cake mix
1 (8-ounce) package cream cheese, softened
2 tablespoons butter or margarine, softened
1 tablespoon cornstarch
1 (14-ounce) can Eagle® Brand Sweetened Condensed Milk (NOT evaporated milk), divided
1 egg
1 teaspoon vanilla extract
  Chocolate Glaze (recipe follows)

1. Preheat oven to 350°F. Grease and flour 13×9-inch baking pan. Prepare cake mix as package directs. Pour batter into prepared pan.

2. In small bowl, beat cream cheese, butter and cornstarch until fluffy. Gradually beat in **Eagle Brand.** Add egg and vanilla; beat until smooth. Spoon evenly over cake batter.

3. Bake 40 minutes or until wooden pick inserted near center comes out clean. Cool. Prepare Chocolate Glaze and drizzle over cake. Store covered in refrigerator.   *Makes 10 to 12 servings*

Chocolate Glaze
In small saucepan over low heat, melt 1 (1-ounce) square unsweetened or semi-sweet chocolate and 1 tablespoon butter or margarine with 2 tablespoons water. Remove from heat. Stir in ¾ cup powdered sugar and ½ teaspoon vanilla extract. Stir until smooth and well blended. Makes about ⅓ cup.

Fudge Ribbon Bundt Cake: Preheat oven to 350°F. Grease and flour 10-inch bundt pan. Prepare cake mix as package directs. Pour batter into prepared pan. Prepare cream cheese topping as directed above; spoon evenly over batter. Bake 50 to 55 minutes or until wooden pick inserted near center comes out clean. Cool 10 minutes. Remove from pan. Cool. Prepare Chocolate Glaze and drizzle over cake. Store covered in refrigerator.

Fudge Ribbon Sheet Cake

Double Chocolate Cookies

Prep Time: 15 minutes   **Bake Time:** 10 minutes

2 cups biscuit baking mix
1 (14-ounce) can Eagle® Brand Sweetened Condensed Milk (NOT evaporated milk)
8 (1-ounce) squares semi-sweet chocolate *or* 1 (12-ounce) package semi-sweet chocolate chips, melted
3 tablespoons butter or margarine, melted
1 egg
1 teaspoon vanilla extract
6 (1¼-ounce) white candy bars with almonds, broken into small pieces
¾ cup chopped nuts

1. Preheat oven to 350°F. In large bowl, combine all ingredients except candy pieces and nuts; beat until smooth.

2. Stir in remaining ingredients. Drop by rounded teaspoonfuls, 2 inches apart, onto ungreased baking sheets.

3. Bake 10 minutes or until tops are slightly crusted (do not overbake). Cool. Store tightly covered at room temperature.

Makes about 4½ dozen

Mint Chocolate Cookies: Substitute ¾ cup mint-flavored chocolate chips for white candy bars with almonds. Proceed as directed above.

Top to bottom: Double Chocolate Cookies and Chocolate Raspberry Truffles (page 46)

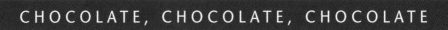

Chocolate Raspberry Truffles

Prep Time: 10 minutes   **Cook Time:** 3 minutes
Chill Time: 1 hour

> **1 (14-ounce) can Eagle® Brand Sweetened Condensed Milk (NOT evaporated milk)**
> **¼ cup raspberry liqueur**
> **2 tablespoons butter or margarine**
> **2 tablespoons seedless raspberry jam**
> **2 (12-ounce) packages semi-sweet chocolate chips**
> **½ cup powdered sugar or crushed toasted almonds**

1. Microwave first 4 ingredients in large microwave-safe bowl on 100% power (HIGH) 3 minutes.

2. Stir in chips until smooth. Cover and chill 1 hour.

3. Shape mixture into 1-inch balls and roll in powdered sugar or almonds. Store covered at room temperature.   *Makes 4 dozen*

 *Helpful Hint*

To measure Eagle Brand easily, remove the entire lid first, and then scrape the Eagle Brand into a glass measuring cup using a rubber scraper.

46

Chocolate-Peanut Butter Mousse Pie

Prep Time: 20 minutes   **Chill Time:** 2 hours

> 1 cup chocolate graham cracker crumbs
> ⅓ cup honey-roasted peanuts, finely chopped
> 6 tablespoons butter or margarine, softened
> 1½ cups whipping cream, divided
> 1 (14-ounce) can Eagle® Brand Sweetened Condensed Milk (NOT evaporated milk), divided
> 1½ cups semi-sweet chocolate chips
> 2 (3-ounce) packages cream cheese, softened
> ¾ cup creamy peanut butter

1. In medium bowl, combine crumbs, peanuts and butter; press mixture in bottom and up side of 9-inch pie plate. Set aside.

2. Pour ½ cup whipping cream into microwave-safe bowl; microwave on 100% power (HIGH) 2 minutes. Stir in ½ cup **Eagle Brand** and chips until smooth. Spoon mixture into prepared crust. Chill 1 hour.

3. In large bowl, beat remaining 1 cup whipping cream until stiff peaks form; set aside. In small bowl, beat remaining **Eagle Brand,** cream cheese and peanut butter until smooth. Fold in ⅓ of whipped cream; fold in remaining whipped cream. Spoon over chocolate filling. Chill 1 hour. Store covered in refrigerator.

Makes 1 (9-inch) pie

Fudge-Filled Bars

Prep Time: 20 minutes   **Bake Time:** 25 to 30 minutes

> 1 (14-ounce) can Eagle® Brand Sweetened Condensed Milk (NOT evaporated milk)
> 1 (12-ounce) package semi-sweet chocolate chips
> 2 tablespoons butter or margarine
> 2 teaspoons vanilla extract
> 2 (18-ounce) packages refrigerated cookie dough (oatmeal-chocolate chip, chocolate chip, or sugar cookie dough)

1. Preheat oven to 350°F. In heavy saucepan over medium heat, combine **Eagle Brand,** chips and butter; heat until chips melt, stirring often. Remove from heat; stir in vanilla. Cool 15 minutes.

2. Using floured hands, press 1½ packages of cookie dough into ungreased 15×10×1-inch baking pan. Pour cooled chocolate mixture evenly over dough. Crumble remaining dough over filling.

3. Bake 25 to 30 minutes. Cool. Cut into bars. Store covered at room temperature.

Makes 48 bars

 *Helpful Hint*

If you want to trim the fat in any Eagle® Brand recipe, just use Eagle® Brand Fat Free or Low Fat Sweetened Condensed Milk instead of the original Eagle Brand.

Fudge-Filled Bars

Any-Day Delights

Scrumptious bars and brownies, a luscious cheesecake or rich fudge is just the thing to turn a ho-hum day into a delight. You will see nothing but smiles when they know that you've made delicious Eagle® Brand treats. Eagle® Brand transforms simple ingredients you keep on hand into extra-special treats. And these goodies and desserts are so simple to make, you won't want to wait for a special occasion. So make any day brighter with the magic of Eagle® Brand.

Clockwise from top right: Peanut Blossom Cookies (page 52), Easy Peanut Butter Cookies (page 52) and Crunchy Clusters (page 53)

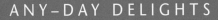

Easy Peanut Butter Cookies

Prep Time: 10 minutes   **Chill Time:** 1 hour

Bake Time: 6 to 8 minutes

> **1 (14-ounce) can Eagle® Brand Sweetened Condensed Milk (NOT evaporated milk)**
> **¾ to 1 cup peanut butter**
> **1 egg**
> **1 teaspoon vanilla extract**
> **2 cups biscuit baking mix**
>   **Sugar**

1. In large bowl, beat **Eagle Brand,** peanut butter, egg and vanilla until smooth. Add biscuit mix; mix well. Chill at least 1 hour.

2. Preheat oven to 350°F. Shape dough into 1-inch balls. Roll in sugar. Place 2 inches apart on ungreased baking sheets.

3. Flatten with fork in criss-cross pattern. Bake 6 to 8 minutes or until lightly browned (do not overbake). Cool. Store tightly covered at room temperature.   *Makes about 5 dozen*

Peanut Blossom Cookies: Make dough as directed above. Shape into 1-inch balls and roll in sugar; do not flatten. Bake as directed above. Immediately after baking, press solid milk chocolate candy drop in center of each ball.

Peanut Butter & Jelly Gems: Make dough as directed above. Shape into 1-inch balls and roll in sugar; do not flatten. Press thumb in center of each ball of dough; fill with jelly, jam or preserves. Proceed as directed above.

Any-Way-You-Like 'em Cookies: Stir 1 cup semi-sweet chocolate chips, chopped peanuts, raisins or flaked coconut into dough. Proceed as directed above.

Crunchy Clusters

Prep Time: 10 minutes   **Chill Time:** 2 hours

> **1 (12-ounce) package semi-sweet chocolate chips** *or* **3 (6-ounce) packages butterscotch-flavored chips**
> **1 (14-ounce) can Eagle® Brand Sweetened Condensed Milk (NOT evaporated milk)**
> **1 (3-ounce) can chow mein noodles** *or* **2 cups pretzel sticks, broken into ½-inch pieces**
> **1 cup dry-roasted peanuts or whole roasted almonds**

1. Line baking sheet with waxed paper. In heavy saucepan over low heat, melt chips with **Eagle Brand.** Remove from heat.

2. In large bowl, combine noodles and peanuts; stir in chocolate mixture.

3. Drop by tablespoonfuls onto prepared baking sheet; chill 2 hours or until firm. Store loosely covered at room temperature.

Makes about 3 dozen

Microwave Directions: In 2-quart glass measure, combine chips and **Eagle Brand.** Cook on 100% power (HIGH) 3 minutes, stirring after 1½ minutes. Stir until smooth. Proceed as directed above.

 *Helpful Hint*

> *Here are some other ways to make any day special with Eagle Brand:*
> - *Offer it as a topper for waffles and French toast.*
> - *Pour it directly into a pretty bowl for a fruit dip.*
> - *Spoon some over cake instead of frosting.*
> - *Stir it into coffee or tea for a coffeehouse-type beverage.*

Microwave Cheesecake

Prep Time: 15 minutes   **Cook Time:** 14½ to 18½ minutes
Chill Time: 3 hours

⅓ cup (⅔ stick) butter or margarine
1¼ cups graham cracker crumbs
¼ cup sugar
2 (8-ounce) packages cream cheese, softened
1 (14-ounce) can Eagle® Brand Sweetened Condensed Milk (NOT evaporated milk)
3 eggs
¼ cup ReaLemon® Lemon Juice from Concentrate
1 (8-ounce) container sour cream, at room temperature

1. In 10-inch microwave-safe quiche dish or pie plate, melt butter loosely covered on 100% power (HIGH) 1 minute. Add crumbs and sugar; press firmly on bottom of dish.

2. Cook on 100% power (HIGH) 1½ minutes, rotating dish once.

3. In 2-quart glass measure, beat cream cheese until fluffy. Gradually beat in **Eagle Brand** until smooth. Add eggs and **ReaLemon;** mix well. Cook on 70% power (MEDIUM-HIGH) 6 to 8 minutes or until hot, stirring every 2 minutes.

4. Pour into prepared crust. Cook on 50% power (MEDIUM) 6 to 8 minutes or until center is set, rotating dish once. Top with sour cream. Cool. Chill 3 hours or until set. Serve or top with fruit, if desired. Store covered in refrigerator.

Makes 1 (10-inch) cheesecake

Microwave Cheesecake

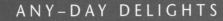

Double Chocolate Fantasy Bars

Prep Time: 15 minutes   **Bake Time:** 25 to 30 minutes

   1 (18¼-ounce) package chocolate cake mix
¼ cup vegetable oil
   1 egg
   1 cup chopped nuts
   1 (14-ounce) can Eagle® Brand Sweetened Condensed Milk (NOT
      evaporated milk)
   1 (6-ounce) package semi-sweet chocolate chips
   1 teaspoon vanilla extract
   Dash salt

1. Preheat oven to 350°F. Grease 13×9-inch baking pan. In large bowl, combine cake mix, oil and egg; beat on medium speed until crumbly. Stir in nuts. Reserve 1½ cups crumb mixture. Press remaining crumb mixture on bottom of prepared pan.

2. In small saucepan over medium heat, combine remaining ingredients. Cook and stir until chips melt.

3. Pour chocolate mixture evenly over prepared crust. Sprinkle reserved crumb mixture evenly over top. Bake 25 to 30 minutes or until set. Cool. Cut into bars. Store loosely covered at room temperature.

Makes 36 bars

 *Helpful Hint*

> Eagle Brand makes great cookies and bars, but don't forget that desserts
> made with Eagle Brand contain condensed all-natural milk. This gives
> your family important bone-building calcium in every bite.

*Top to bottom: Double Chocolate Fantasy
Bars and Toffee Bars (page 58)*

Toffee Bars

Prep Time: 45 minutes   Bake Time: 20 to 30 minutes
Cook Time: 15 minutes

  1 cup oats
  ½ cup packed brown sugar
  ½ cup all-purpose flour
  ½ cup finely chopped walnuts
  ½ cup (1 stick) butter or margarine, melted and divided
  ¼ teaspoon baking soda
  1 (14-ounce) can Eagle® Brand Sweetened Condensed Milk (NOT
     evaporated milk)
  2 teaspoons vanilla extract
  1 (6-ounce) package semi-sweet chocolate chips

1. Preheat oven to 350°F. Grease 13×9-inch baking pan. Combine oats, sugar, flour, walnuts, 6 tablespoons butter and baking soda. Press firmly on bottom of prepared pan. Bake 10 to 15 minutes or until lightly browned.

2. Meanwhile, in medium saucepan over medium heat, combine remaining 2 tablespoons butter and **Eagle Brand.** Cook and stir until mixture thickens slightly, about 15 minutes. Remove from heat; stir in vanilla. Pour over baked crust.

3. Bake 10 to 15 minutes or until golden brown.

4. Remove from oven; immediately sprinkle chips on top. Let stand 1 minute; spread chips while still warm. Cool. Cut into bars. Store tightly covered at room temperature.   *Makes 36 bars*

Quick No-Bake Brownies

Prep Time: 15 minutes   Chill Time: 4 hours

  1 cup finely chopped nuts, divided
  2 (1-ounce) squares unsweetened chocolate
  1 (14-ounce) can Eagle® Brand Sweetened Condensed Milk (NOT
     evaporated milk)
  2 to 2½ cups vanilla wafer crumbs (about 48 to 60 wafers)

1. Grease 9-inch square pan with butter. Sprinkle ¼ cup nuts evenly in bottom of pan. In heavy saucepan over low heat, melt chocolate with **Eagle Brand.** Cook and stir until mixture thickens, about 10 minutes.

2. Remove from heat; stir in crumbs and ½ cup nuts. Spread evenly into prepared pan.

3. Top with remaining ¼ cup nuts. Chill 4 hours or until firm. Cut into squares. Store loosely covered at room temperature.

Makes 24 brownies

Butterscotch Apple Squares

Prep Time: 15 minutes **Bake Time:** 25 to 30 minutes

   ¼ **cup (½ stick) butter or margarine**
 1½ **cups graham cracker crumbs**
   2 **small all-purpose apples, pared and chopped (about 1¼ cups)**
   1 **(6-ounce) package butterscotch-flavored chips**
   1 **(14-ounce) can Eagle® Brand Sweetened Condensed Milk (NOT evaporated milk)**
 1⅓ **cups flaked coconut**
   1 **cup chopped nuts**

1. Preheat oven to 350°F (325°F for glass dish). In 13×9-inch baking pan, melt butter in oven. Sprinkle crumbs evenly over butter; top with apples.

2. In heavy saucepan over medium heat, melt chips with **Eagle Brand.** Pour butterscotch mixture evenly over apples. Top with coconut and nuts; press down firmly.

3. Bake 25 to 30 minutes or until lightly browned. Cool. Cut into squares. Store covered in refrigerator. *Makes 12 servings*

Cookies 'n' Crème Fudge

Prep Time: 10 minutes   **Chill Time:** 2 hours

 3 (6-ounce) packages white chocolate baking squares
 1 (14-ounce) can Eagle® Brand Sweetened Condensed Milk (NOT evaporated milk)
 ⅛ teaspoon salt
 2 cups coarsely crushed chocolate crème-filled sandwich cookies (about 20 cookies)

1. Line 8-inch square baking pan with foil. In heavy saucepan over low heat, melt chocolate with **Eagle Brand** and salt. Remove from heat. Stir in crushed cookies. Spread evenly in prepared pan. Chill 2 hours or until firm.

2. Turn fudge onto cutting board. Peel off foil; cut into squares. Store tightly covered at room temperature.   *Makes about 2½ pounds*

No-Bake Peanutty Chocolate Drops

Prep Time: 10 minutes   **Chill Time:** 2 hours

 ½ cup (1 stick) butter or margarine
 ⅓ cup unsweetened cocoa
 1 (14-ounce) can Eagle® Brand Sweetened Condensed Milk (NOT evaporated milk)
 2½ cups quick-cooking oats
 1 cup chopped peanuts
 ½ cup peanut butter

1. Line baking sheets with waxed paper. In medium saucepan over medium heat, melt butter; stir in cocoa. Bring mixture to a boil.

2. Remove from heat; stir in remaining ingredients.

3. Drop by teaspoonfuls onto prepared baking sheets; chill 2 hours or until set. Store loosely covered in refrigerator.

Makes about 5 dozen

Cookies 'n' Crème Fudge

Candy Bar Bars

Prep Time: 20 minutes   **Bake Time:** 40 minutes

¾ cup (1½ sticks) butter or margarine, softened
¼ cup peanut butter
1 cup packed brown sugar
1 teaspoon baking soda
2 cups quick-cooking oats
1½ cups all-purpose flour
1 egg
1 (14-ounce) can Eagle® Brand Sweetened Condensed Milk (NOT evaporated milk)
4 cups chopped candy bars (such as chocolate-coated caramel-topped nougat bars with peanuts, chocolate-covered crisp wafers, chocolate-covered caramel-topped cookie bars, or chocolate-covered peanut butter cups)

1. Preheat oven to 350°F. In large bowl, combine butter and peanut butter. Add sugar and baking soda; beat well. Stir in oats and flour. Reserve 1¾ cups crumb mixture.

2. Stir egg into remaining crumb mixture; press firmly on bottom of ungreased 15×10×1-inch baking pan. Bake 15 minutes.

3. Spread **Eagle Brand** over baked crust. Stir together reserved crumb mixture and candy bar pieces; sprinkle evenly over top. Bake 25 minutes or until golden. Cool. Cut into bars. Store covered at room temperature.   *Makes 48 bars*

Candy Bar Bars

Luscious Homemade Gifts

*W*hat better way to show you care than to make a mouth-watering goodie that everyone can enjoy. Whether it's to say "Happy Holidays," "Welcome to the Neighborhood" or "Thank You," nothing says it sweeter and easier than these magical cookies, incredible bars and festive candies. Best of all, because these sweets are made with Eagle® Brand and made by you, they're the best gift you can give. Eagle® Brand makes "homemade"…magic.

Top to bottom: Chocolate Pecan Critters (page 66), Peanut Butter Fudge (page 66) and Layered Mint Chocolate Candy (page 67)

64

Chocolate Pecan Critters

Prep Time: 10 minutes

> 1 (11½-ounce) package milk chocolate chips
> 1 (6-ounce) package semi-sweet chocolate chips
> ¼ cup (½ stick) butter or margarine
> 1 (14-ounce) can Eagle® Brand Sweetened Condensed Milk (NOT evaporated milk)
> ⅛ teaspoon salt
> 2 cups coarsely chopped pecans
> 2 teaspoons vanilla extract
> Pecan halves

1. Line baking sheets with waxed paper. In heavy saucepan over medium heat, melt chips and butter with **Eagle Brand** and salt.

2. Remove from heat; stir in chopped pecans and vanilla.

3. Drop by spoonfuls onto prepared baking sheets. Top with pecan halves. Chill. Store tightly covered at room temperature.

Makes about 5 dozen

Microwave Directions: In 2-quart glass measure, microwave chips, butter, **Eagle Brand** and salt on 100% power (HIGH) 3 minutes. Stir after 1½ minutes. Stir to melt chips; add chopped pecans and vanilla. Proceed as directed above.

Peanut Butter Fudge

Prep Time: 5 minutes   Cook Time: 4 to 5 minutes
Chill Time: 2 hours

> 2 (10-ounce) packages peanut butter-flavored chips
> 1 (14-ounce) can Eagle® Brand Sweetened Condensed Milk (NOT evaporated milk)
> ¼ cup (½ stick) butter or margarine, cut into pieces
> 1 cup chopped salted peanuts

1. Butter 8-inch square dish. Microwave first 3 ingredients in a 2-quart microwave-safe bowl at 50% power (MEDIUM) 4 to 5 minutes, stirring at 1½-minute intervals.

2. Stir in peanuts and pour into prepared dish. Cover and chill 2 hours. Cut into squares. Store covered in refrigerator.

Makes 2 pounds

Layered Mint Chocolate Candy

Prep Time: 20 minutes   **Chill Time:** 2 hours 20 minutes

1 (12-ounce) package semi-sweet chocolate chips
1 (14-ounce) can Eagle® Brand Sweetened Condensed Milk (NOT evaporated milk), divided
2 teaspoons vanilla extract
1 cup (6 ounces) deluxe white baking chips
1 tablespoon peppermint extract
    Few drops green or red food coloring (optional)

1. Line 8- or 9-inch square pan with waxed paper. In heavy saucepan over low heat, melt semi-sweet chips with 1 cup **Eagle Brand.** Stir in vanilla. Spread half the mixture in prepared pan; chill 10 minutes or until firm. Keep remaining chocolate mixture at room temperature.

2. In heavy saucepan over low heat, melt white chips with remaining **Eagle Brand.** Stir in peppermint extract and food coloring. Spread over chilled chocolate layer; chill 10 minutes or until firm. Spread reserved chocolate mixture over mint layer. Chill 2 hours or until firm.

3. Turn candy onto cutting board; peel off paper and cut into squares. Store loosely covered at room temperature.

Makes about 1¾ pounds

Triple Chocolate Cheesecakes

Prep Time: 20 minutes   Chill Time: 4 hours

- 1 envelope unflavored gelatin
- ½ cup cold water
- 1 (14-ounce) can Eagle® Brand Sweetened Condensed Milk (NOT evaporated milk)
- 2 (8-ounce) packages cream cheese, softened
- 4 (1-ounce) squares unsweetened chocolate, melted and slightly cooled
- 1 (8-ounce) carton frozen non-dairy whipped topping, thawed
- ½ cup (3 ounces) mini chocolate chips
- 1 (21-ounce) can cherry pie filling (optional)
- 2 (6-ounce) ready-made chocolate crumb pie crusts

1. In 1-cup glass measure, stir together gelatin and cold water; let stand 5 minutes to soften. Pour about 1 inch water into small saucepan; place glass measure in saucepan. Place saucepan over medium heat; stir until gelatin is dissolved. Remove measure from saucepan; cool slightly.

2. In large bowl, combine **Eagle Brand,** cream cheese and melted chocolate; beat until smooth. Gradually beat in gelatin mixture. Fold in whipped topping and chips.

3. Spread pie filling on bottoms of crusts, if desired. Spoon chocolate mixture into pie crusts. Cover and chill at least 4 hours. Store covered in refrigerator.   *Makes 2 cheesecakes (12 servings total)*

Tip: To store this cheesecake in the freezer, cover and freeze up to 1 month. Serve frozen, or remove from freezer several hours before serving and let thaw in the refrigerator.

Triple Chocolate Cheesecake

Double Chocolate Cherry Cookies

Prep Time: 25 minutes   **Bake Time:** 8 to 10 minutes

1¼ cups (2½ sticks) butter or margarine, softened
1¾ cups sugar
  2 eggs
  1 tablespoon vanilla extract
3½ cups all-purpose flour
  ¾ cup unsweetened cocoa
  ½ teaspoon baking powder
  ½ teaspoon baking soda
  ¼ teaspoon salt
  2 (6-ounce) jars maraschino cherries, well drained and halved
      (about 60 cherries)
  1 (6-ounce) package semi-sweet chocolate chips
  1 (14-ounce) can Eagle® Brand Sweetened Condensed Milk (NOT
      evaporated milk)

1. Preheat oven to 350°F. In large bowl, beat butter and sugar until fluffy. Add eggs and vanilla; mix well.

2. In large bowl, combine dry ingredients; stir into butter mixture (dough will be stiff). Shape into 1-inch balls. Place 1 inch apart on ungreased baking sheets.

3. Press cherry half into center of each cookie. Bake 8 to 10 minutes. Cool.

4. In heavy saucepan over medium heat, melt chips with **Eagle Brand;** cook until mixture thickens, about 3 minutes. Frost each cookie, covering cherry. Store loosely covered at room temperature.
Makes about 10 dozen

Double Chocolate Pecan Cookies: Prepare and shape dough as directed above, omitting cherries. Flatten. Bake and frost as directed. Garnish each cookie with pecan half.

Easy Chocolate Truffles

Prep Time: 10 minutes   **Chill Time:** 3 hours

3 (6-ounce) packages semi-sweet chocolate chips
1 (14-ounce) can Eagle® Brand Sweetened Condensed Milk (NOT evaporated milk)
1 tablespoon vanilla extract
  Coatings: finely chopped nuts, flaked coconut, chocolate sprinkles, colored sprinkles, unsweetened cocoa or colored sugar

1. In heavy saucepan over low heat, melt chips with **Eagle Brand.** Remove from heat; stir in vanilla.

2. Chill 2 hours or until firm. Shape into 1-inch balls; roll in desired coating.

3. Chill 1 hour or until firm. Store covered at room temperature.

Makes about 6 dozen

Microwave Directions: In 1-quart measure, combine chips and **Eagle Brand.** Cook on 100% power (HIGH) 3 minutes, stirring after 1½ minutes. Stir until smooth. Proceed as directed above.

Amaretto Truffles: Substitute 3 tablespoons amaretto liqueur and ½ teaspoon almond extract for vanilla. Roll in finely chopped toasted almonds.

Orange Truffles: Substitute 3 tablespoons orange-flavored liqueur for vanilla. Roll in finely chopped toasted almonds mixed with finely grated orange rind.

Rum Truffles: Substitute ¼ cup dark rum for vanilla. Roll in flaked coconut.

Bourbon Truffles: Substitute 3 tablespoons bourbon for vanilla. Roll in finely chopped toasted nuts.

Chocolate Peanut Butter Dessert Sauce

Prep Time: 15 minutes

> 2 (1-ounce) squares semi-sweet chocolate, chopped
> 2 tablespoons creamy peanut butter
> 1 (14-ounce) can Eagle® Brand Sweetened Condensed Milk (NOT
>   evaporated milk)
> 2 tablespoons milk
> 1 teaspoon vanilla extract

1. In medium saucepan over medium-low heat, melt chocolate and peanut butter with **Eagle Brand** and milk, stirring constantly.

2. Remove from heat; stir in vanilla. Cool slightly. Serve warm over ice cream, cake or as fruit dipping sauce. Store covered in refrigerator.   *Makes about 1½ cups*

Coconut Macaroons

Prep Time: 10 minutes   Bake Time: 15 to 17 minutes

> 1 (14-ounce) can Eagle® Brand Sweetened Condensed Milk (NOT
>   evaporated milk)
> 2 teaspoons vanilla extract
> 1 to 1½ teaspoons almond extract
> 2 (7-ounce) packages flaked coconut (5⅓ cups)

1. Preheat oven to 325°F. Line baking sheets with foil; grease and flour foil. Set aside.

2. In large bowl, combine **Eagle Brand,** vanilla and almond extract. Stir in coconut. Drop by rounded teaspoons onto prepared sheets; with spoon, slightly flatten each mound.

3. Bake 15 to 17 minutes or until golden. Remove from baking sheets; cool on wire rack. Store loosely covered at room temperature.
Makes about 4 dozen

Chocolate Peanut Butter Dessert Sauce

Chocolate Streusel Bars

Prep Time: 15 minutes Bake Time: 40 minutes

1¾ cups all-purpose flour
1½ cups powdered sugar
½ cup unsweetened cocoa
1 cup (2 sticks) cold butter or margarine
1 (8-ounce) package cream cheese, softened
1 (14-ounce) can Eagle® Brand Sweetened Condensed Milk (NOT evaporated milk)
1 egg
2 teaspoons vanilla extract
½ cup chopped walnuts

1. Preheat oven to 350°F. In large bowl, combine flour, sugar and cocoa; cut in butter until crumbly (mixture will be dry). Reserve 2 cups crumb mixture. Press remaining crumb mixture firmly on bottom of ungreased 13×9-inch baking pan. Bake 15 minutes.

2. Meanwhile, in large bowl, beat cream cheese until fluffy. Gradually beat in **Eagle Brand** until smooth. Add egg and vanilla; mix well. Pour evenly over baked crust.

3. Combine reserved crumb mixture with walnuts; sprinkle evenly over cheese mixture. Bake 25 minutes or until bubbly. Cool. Chill. Cut into bars. Store covered in refrigerator.   *Makes 24 to 36 bars*

Pecan Pie Bars

Prep Time: 15 minutes Bake Time: 40 minutes

2 cups all-purpose flour
½ cup powdered sugar
1 cup (2 sticks) cold butter or margarine
1 (14-ounce) can Eagle® Brand Sweetened Condensed Milk (NOT evaporated milk)
1 egg
1 teaspoon vanilla extract
1 (6-ounce) package almond brickle chips
1 cup chopped pecans

1. Preheat oven to 350°F (325°F for glass dish). In medium bowl, combine flour and sugar; cut in butter until crumbly. Press firmly on bottom of ungreased 13×9-inch baking pan. Bake 15 minutes.

2. Meanwhile, in medium bowl, beat **Eagle Brand,** egg and vanilla. Stir in chips and pecans. Spread evenly over baked crust.

3. Bake 25 minutes or until golden brown. Cool. Chill thoroughly. Cut into bars. Store covered in refrigerator. *Makes 36 bars*

Chocolate Almond Brownies

Prep Time: 15 minutes   **Bake Time:** 45 minutes

  1¼ **cups all-purpose flour, divided**
   2 **tablespoons sugar**
  ½ **cup (1 stick) cold butter or margarine**
   1 **cup chopped almonds, toasted and divided**
   1 **(14-ounce) can Eagle® Brand Sweetened Condensed Milk (NOT**
     evaporated milk)
  ¼ **cup unsweetened cocoa**
   1 **egg**
   2 **tablespoons amaretto liqueur *or* 1 teaspoon almond extract**
  ½ **teaspoon baking powder**
   6 **(1¼-ounce) white candy bars with almonds, broken into small**
     pieces

1. Preheat oven to 350°F. In medium bowl, combine 1 cup flour and sugar; cut in butter until crumbly. Add ¼ cup almonds. Press firmly on bottom of ungreased 9-inch round or square baking pan. Bake 15 minutes.

2. In large bowl, beat **Eagle Brand,** remaining ¼ cup flour, cocoa, egg, amaretto and baking powder until smooth. Stir in candy pieces and ½ cup almonds. Spread over baked crust.

3. Top with remaining ¼ cup almonds. Bake 30 minutes or until center is set. Cool. Cut into wedges. Store tightly covered at room temperature. *Makes 16 brownies*

Let's Celebrate

Celebrations mean having parties for holidays, family gatherings, birthdays and anniversaries, to name a few. With Eagle® Brand magic there's plenty of time to mingle because you can make party-perfect treats ahead of time, in no time. Simply make three or four of the fantastic desserts and treats in this chapter and then, at party time, mix up a batch of your favorite Eagle® Brand beverage. Refreshments are served and you'll be celebrating . . . Enjoy.

Top to bottom: Festive Cranberry Cream Punch (page 78) and Party Mints (page 79)

Festive Cranberry Cream Punch

Prep Time: 5 minutes

> 1 (14-ounce) can Eagle® Brand Sweetened Condensed Milk (NOT evaporated milk)
> 1 (12-ounce) can frozen cranberry juice cocktail concentrate, thawed
> 1 cup cranberry-flavored liqueur (optional)
>   Red food coloring (optional)
> 2 (1-liter) bottles club soda or ginger ale, chilled
>   Cranberry Ice Ring (recipe follows, optional) or ice

1. In punch bowl, combine **Eagle Brand,** concentrate, liqueur and food coloring.

2. Just before serving, add club soda and Cranberry Ice Ring or ice. Store tightly covered in refrigerator.

3. Prepare Cranberry Ice Ring, if desired, one day in advance, or use ice.   *Makes about 3 quarts*

Cranberry Ice Ring

>   2 cups cranberry juice cocktail
> 1½ cups water
>   ¾ to 1 cup cranberries and lime slices or mint leaves

1. Combine cranberry juice cocktail and water. In 1½-quart ring mold, pour ½ cup cranberry liquid.

2. Arrange cranberries and lime slices or mint leaves in mold; freeze.

3. Add remaining 3 cups cranberry liquid to mold; freeze.

Party Mints

Prep Time: 30 minutes   Stand Time: 8 hours

> 1 (14-ounce) can Eagle® Brand Sweetened Condensed Milk (NOT evaporated milk)
> 1 (32-ounce) package powdered sugar
> ½ teaspoon peppermint extract
>   Assorted colored granulated sugar or crystals

1. In medium bowl, beat **Eagle Brand** and half of powdered sugar until blended. Gradually add remaining powdered sugar and peppermint extract, beating until stiff.

2. Roll mixture into ½-inch balls; roll in desired sugar and place on lightly greased cooling rack. Let stand 8 hours. Store covered at room temperature.   *Makes 2½ pounds*

Streusel Caramel Bars

Prep Time: 25 minutes   Bake Time: 35 minutes

> 2 cups all-purpose flour
> ¾ cup packed brown sugar
> 1 egg, beaten
> ¾ cup (1½ sticks) cold butter or margarine, divided
> ¾ cup chopped nuts
> 24 caramels, unwrapped
> 1 (14-ounce) can Eagle® Brand Sweetened Condensed Milk (NOT evaporated milk)

1. Preheat oven to 350°F. Grease 13×9-inch baking pan. In large bowl, combine flour, sugar and egg; cut in ½ cup butter until crumbly. Stir in nuts. Reserve 2 cups crumb mixture. Press remaining crumb mixture firmly on bottom of prepared pan. Bake 15 minutes.

2. Meanwhile, in heavy saucepan over low heat, melt caramels and remaining ¼ cup butter with **Eagle Brand.** Pour over baked crust.

3. Top with reserved crumb mixture. Bake 20 minutes or until bubbly. Cool. Cut into bars. Store loosely covered at room temperature.   *Makes 24 to 36 bars*

Chocolate Almond Torte

Prep Time: 30 minutes   **Bake Time:** 18 to 20 minutes

    4 eggs, separated
    ½ cup (1 stick) butter or margarine, softened
    1 cup sugar
    1 teaspoon vanilla extract
    1 teaspoon almond extract
    1 cup finely chopped toasted almonds
    ¾ cup all-purpose flour
    ½ cup unsweetened cocoa
    ½ teaspoon baking powder
    ½ teaspoon baking soda
    ⅔ cup milk
    Chocolate Almond Frosting (page 82)

1. Line 2 (8- or 9-inch) round cake pans with waxed paper. Preheat oven to 350°F. In small bowl, beat egg whites until soft peaks form; set aside.

2. In large bowl, beat butter and sugar until fluffy. Add egg yolks and extracts; mix well.

3. In medium bowl, combine almonds, flour, cocoa, baking powder and baking soda; add alternately with milk to butter mixture, beating well after each addition.

4. Fold in beaten egg whites. Pour into prepared pans. Bake 18 to 20 minutes or until wooden pick inserted near center comes out clean. Cool 10 minutes; remove from pans. Cool completely.

5. Prepare Chocolate Almond Frosting. Split each cake layer; fill and frost with frosting. Garnish as desired. Store covered in refrigerator.

Makes 1 (4-layer) cake

continued on page 82

Chocolate Almond Torte

Chocolate Almond Torte, continued

Chocolate Almond Frosting

Prep Time: 20 minutes

> **2 (1-ounce) squares semi-sweet chocolate, chopped**
> **1 (14-ounce) can Eagle® Brand Sweetened Condensed Milk (NOT evaporated milk)**
> **1 teaspoon almond extract**

1. In heavy saucepan over medium heat, melt chocolate with **Eagle Brand.** Cook and stir until mixture thickens, about 10 minutes.

2. Remove from heat; cool 10 minutes. Stir in almond extract; cool.

Makes about 1½ cups

Chewy Almond Squares

Prep Time: 10 minutes   **Bake Time:** 30 to 37 minutes

> **1¼ cups graham cracker crumbs**
> **¼ cup sugar**
> **⅓ cup (⅔ stick) butter or margarine, melted**
> **1 cup flaked coconut, toasted**
> **1 cup chopped almonds, toasted***
> **1 (14-ounce) can Eagle® Brand Sweetened Condensed Milk (NOT evaporated milk)**

*1 cup chopped pecans or walnuts, toasted, may be substituted.

1. Preheat oven to 375°F. Line 9-inch square pan with foil. In medium bowl, combine crumbs, sugar and butter. Press into bottom of prepared pan. Bake 5 to 7 minutes.

2. Sprinkle crust with coconut and almonds; pour **Eagle Brand** evenly over surface.

3. Bake 25 to 30 minutes. Cool on wire rack. Cut into squares. Store covered at room temperature.

Makes 16 squares

Top to bottom: Chewy Almond Squares and Marbled Cheesecake Bars (page 89)

German Chocolate Cake

Prep Time: 15 minutes   **Bake Time:** 40 to 45 minutes

- 1 (18¼-ounce) package chocolate cake mix
- 1 cup water
- 3 eggs plus 1 egg yolk
- ½ cup vegetable oil
- 1 (14-ounce) can Eagle® Brand Sweetened Condensed Milk (NOT evaporated milk), divided
- 3 tablespoons butter or margarine
- ⅓ cup chopped pecans
- ⅓ cup flaked coconut
- 1 teaspoon vanilla extract

1. Preheat oven to 350°F. Grease and flour 13×9-inch baking pan. In large bowl, combine cake mix, water, 3 eggs, oil and ⅓ cup **Eagle Brand.** Beat on low speed until moistened; beat on high speed 2 minutes.

2. Pour into prepared pan. Bake 40 to 45 minutes or until wooden pick inserted near center comes out clean.

3. In small saucepan over medium heat, combine remaining **Eagle Brand,** egg yolk and butter. Cook and stir until thickened, about 6 minutes. Add pecans, coconut and vanilla; spread over warm cake. Store covered in refrigerator.   *Makes 10 to 12 servings*

German Chocolate Cake

Deep Dish Mocha Tiramisu

Prep Time: 15 minutes   Bake Time: 13 to 14 minutes

    1 (14-ounce) can Eagle® Brand Sweetened Condensed Milk (NOT
        evaporated milk), divided
    1 (18.25-ounce) package chocolate cake mix with pudding
    1 cup water
    2 large eggs
    ½ cup vegetable oil
    ½ cup coffee liqueur
        Creamy Coffee Filling (page 88)
        Espresso Sauce (page 88)
        Chocolate-covered coffee beans

1. Preheat oven to 350°F. Grease 5 (8-inch) round cake pans. Reserve
¼ cup **Eagle Brand** for Creamy Coffee Filling.

2. In large bowl, beat ¾ cup **Eagle Brand,** cake mix, water, eggs and
oil until blended. Pour 1 cup batter into each prepared pan.

3. Bake at 350°F for 13 to 14 minutes. Cool in pans on wire racks 10
minutes. Remove from pans; cool completely on wire racks. Prepare
Creamy Coffee Filling and Espresso Sauce.

4. Brush each cake layer evenly with liqueur. Place 1 layer in 4-quart
trifle dish or bowl; top with 1½ cups Creamy Coffee Filling. Drizzle
with ½ cup Espresso Sauce. Repeat procedure with remaining cake
layers, 1 cup chocolate filling, and ¼ cup sauce, ending with cake
layer. Garnish with chocolate-covered coffee beans. Chill. Store
covered in refrigerator.   *Makes 12 servings*

continued on page 88

Deep Dish Mocha Tiramisu

Deep Dish Mocha Tiramisu, continued

Creamy Coffee Filling

Prep Time: 10 minutes

> ¼ cup reserved Eagle® Brand Sweetened Condensed Milk
>   (NOT evaporated milk)
> 1 (8-ounce) package cream cheese, softened
> 2 tablespoons coffee liqueur
> 1½ cups whipping cream

In large bowl, beat first 3 ingredients until blended, about 4 minutes. Add whipping cream and beat until stiff peaks form. Chill, if desired. *Makes 4½ cups*

Espresso Sauce

Prep Time: 10 minutes

> 1 cup water
> ½ cup ground espresso
> 1 (14-ounce) can Eagle® Brand Sweetened Condensed Milk (NOT
>   evaporated milk)
> ¼ cup (½ stick) butter or margarine

In small saucepan over medium heat, bring 1 cup water and ground espresso to a boil. Remove from heat and let stand 5 minutes. Pour mixture through fine wire-mesh strainer; discard grounds. In small saucepan over medium heat, combine espresso and **Eagle Brand.** Bring to a boil. Remove from heat, stir in butter. Cool. *Makes 1¼ cups*

Marbled Cheesecake Bars

Prep Time: 20 minutes   Bake Time: 45 to 50 minutes

> 2 cups finely crushed crème-filled chocolate sandwich cookies (about 24 cookies)
> 3 tablespoons butter or margarine, melted
> 3 (8-ounce) packages cream cheese, softened
> 1 (14-ounce) can Eagle® Brand Sweetened Condensed Milk (NOT evaporated milk)
> 3 eggs
> 2 teaspoons vanilla extract
> 2 (1-ounce) squares unsweetened chocolate, melted

1. Preheat oven to 300°F. Combine crumbs and butter; press firmly on bottom of ungreased 13×9-inch baking pan.

2. In large bowl, beat cream cheese until fluffy. Gradually beat in **Eagle Brand** until smooth. Add eggs and vanilla; mix well. Pour half the batter evenly over prepared crust.

3. Stir melted chocolate into remaining batter; spoon over vanilla batter. With table knife or metal spatula, gently swirl through batter to marble.

4. Bake 45 to 50 minutes or until set. Cool. Chill. Cut into bars. Store covered in refrigerator.   *Makes 24 to 36 bars*

 *Helpful Hint*

For best distribution of added ingredients (chocolate chips, nuts, etc.) or for even marbling, do not oversoften or overbeat the cream cheese.

Raspberry Almond Trifles

Prep Time: 20 minutes   **Chill Time:** 2 hours

> 2 cups whipping cream
> ¼ cup plus 1 tablespoon raspberry liqueur or orange juice, divided
> 1 (14-ounce) can Eagle® Brand Original or Fat Free Sweetened Condensed Milk (NOT evaporated milk)
> 2 (3-ounce) packages ladyfingers, separated
> 1 cup seedless raspberry jam
> ½ cup sliced almonds, toasted

1. In large bowl, beat whipping cream and 1 tablespoon liqueur until stiff peaks form. Fold in **Eagle Brand;** set aside.

2. Layer bottom of 12 (4-ounce) custard cups or ramekins with ladyfingers. Brush with some remaining liqueur. Spread half of jam over ladyfingers. Spread evenly with half of cream mixture; sprinkle with half of almonds. Repeat layers with remaining ladyfingers, liqueur, jam, cream mixture and almonds. Cover and chill 2 hours. Store covered in refrigerator.   *Makes 12 servings*

 *Helpful Hint*

> *To make a simple party more festive, tie ribbons onto stems of glasses, add a fresh bowl of flowers floating in water, and light a few candles at the dinner or dessert table. Enjoy!*

Raspberry Almond Trifles

Chocolate Chip Cheesecake

Prep Time: 15 minutes   **Bake Time:** 35 minutes

   2 (3-ounce) packages cream cheese, softened
   1 (14-ounce) can Eagle® Brand Sweetened Condensed Milk (NOT
      evaporated milk)
   1 egg
   1 teaspoon vanilla extract
   1 cup mini chocolate chips
   1 teaspoon all-purpose flour
   1 (6-ounce) ready-made chocolate crumb pie crust
      Chocolate Glaze (recipe follows)

1. Preheat oven to 350°F. In medium bowl, beat cream cheese until
fluffy. Gradually beat in **Eagle Brand** until smooth. Add egg and
vanilla; mix well.

2. Coat chips with flour; stir into cheese mixture. Pour into crust.

3. Bake 35 minutes or until center springs back when lightly
touched. Cool. Prepare Chocolate Glaze and spread over cheesecake.
Serve chilled. Store covered in refrigerator.   *Makes 6 to 8 servings*

Chocolate Glaze
In small saucepan over low heat, melt ½ cup mini chocolate chips
with ¼ cup whipping cream. Cook and stir until thickened and
smooth. Use immediately.

Index